No More Drama
A Lesson For A Lifetime

Linda Allen Caldwell

No More Drama
A Lesson For A Life Time

Copyright © 2015
Linda Allen Caldwell

*Unless otherwise indicated, all Scripture quotations are from the King
James Version of the Bible.*

ISBN: 978-0-9861274-0-3

FOR INFORMATION CONTACT:
Linda Allen Caldwell
1916 Youree Drive
SHREVEPORT, LA 71101
318-762-8778

E-mail address: mrscaldwellqueen@yahoo.com
Email ordering is available for all books

Printed in the USA by
Morris Publishing®
3212 Hwy. 30E ·Kearney, NE 68847
800-650-7888 www.morrispublishing.com

Dedication

I dedicate this book to my children, so they want have to go through what I had to go through in possessing the spirit of unbelief. I hope this book will instill in them the art of being persistent in believing God's word for all things and teach them how to be consistent in studying the word of God.

•

It was my mother who taught me how to read the Bible persistently, and it was my father who taught me how to be a consistent church member. However, it was my pastor who taught me how to apply the word of God to my life. As an inspirational speaker and writer, I pray I will have a positive impact on many other individuals' lives as my parents and my pastor had on mine.

ACKNOWLEDGEMENTS

I would like to dedicate this book to my entire
immediate family and all other love ones and friends
who have the spirit of UNBELIEF
First of all I would like to thank God for drawing me to
the ministry at Greenwood Acres Full Gospel Baptist
Church where Bishop Fred A. Caldwell Sr. is the
pastor. Bishop, I thank God that he revealed to you a
problem that I didn't even know that I had! As a result
of this revelation, I was inspired to write this book and
share this revelation with all readers, who have an ear
to hear and a heart to receive. I would like to thank my
children and sister for encouraging me to write and
buying me my first engraved writer's journal. Also, I
would like to thank my sister, Betty for being so very,
very patient with me and helping me with all of her
computer skills and critiquing.

Contents

In Memory of My Loving Husband

Introduction

Wow! Here we are in this Great Big World, that I will call a Stage!
Guess What?
We are all Actors going about our daily lives interacting with ourselves and others.

But, the question today Ladies and Gentlemen, Boys and Girls is, ARE YOU A DRAMA KING OR DRAMA QUEEN?

CUT…..TAKE 5…..Now before you get "INSULTED" by being called a DRAMA KING OR DRAMA QUEEN, just as I did before writing this book, come go with me and watch the play unfold to see if you really are a DRAMA KING OR DRAMA QUEEN and what causes or qualifies you to become one.

NO MORE DRAMA
A LESSON FOR A LIFE TIME

Act one
DRAMA BEGINS

LIGHTS…..CAMERA…..ACTION…..It all began the Summer of 2006, when on various occasions during Wednesday Night Bible Study at my church, as well as Sunday Morning Intercessory Prayer Service, including Eleven A.M. Morning Service and finally Six P.M. Night Service, I would go before the church and ask for prayer for my husband, who is an alcoholic. Although, I love my husband, his addiction to alcohol and all the pressures that come along with it, was wearing me out seemingly more than my husband! I must add, my husband is at the age of 55 years old and has been a severe alcoholic for 6 years of our forty one years of marriage. Also, my husband has refused treatment and states that he likes to drink and he's not ready to stop!

Look Out! Here comes the "DRAMA"! I started: worrying and fussing; getting mad, being glad; being happy, being sad; crying and smiling; leaving and returning; criticizing and encouraging; losing sleep, oversleeping; stressing and relaxing; blood pressure elevating, blood pressure too low; heart rate up, heart rate down; confessing and believing; asking for prayers from all the saints at all times, at all church services and whenever the church door opened!!! All that "DRAMA" Can't you see it? I was literally wearing myself out trying to persuade my husband to stop drinking!

Needless to say, it doesn't take a "rocket scientist" to figure out that even though my husband was the alcoholic, I had all the symptoms of an alcoholic: DEPRESSION, ANXIETY, HOPELESSNESS, FATIQUE, STRESS AND DESPAIR! I had been going through more changes than Clark Kent changing into his Superman Suit.

Meanwhile, my husband kept on Drinking, kept on Enjoying it and kept on taking his Alcoholic Naps and waking up Refreshed to Start All Over Again!

Act Two
A Talk with the Preacher

Surprisingly, one evening as I was cleaning the church's sanctuary, which by the way is my daily occupation, Bishop Caldwell, as he sat in his office spoke to me and said, "Hello, Linda, I'm praying for you." Gratefully I returned the greeting but wondered in my mind, why, did he say he was praying for me and not for my husband. Invariably, I needed prayer, but my husband was the Alcoholic and not me! Again, my mind started to wonder, "Did Bishop know something that I didn't know?"

Nevertheless, I stopped for a few minutes in the Bishop's office to thank him for his prayers. Once again the opportunity presented itself for me to speak with him concerning my husband and his addiction.

During the course of our conversation, Bishop Caldwell must have seen on my face, fatigue and despair! Certainly he knew all the times I had been before the congregation for prayer, because he was there praying too! Next, Bishop looked at me and said, "You are tired." My reply was, "No I'm not tired Bishop." Silly me! I was tired of all I was trying to do to help my husband overcome his addiction and didn't realize that it was showing on my face. Lastly, Bishop asked me two questions: "Do you love Jesus?" My reply was, "Yes Bishop I love Jesus." And "Do you trust Jesus?" My reply was, "Yes Bishop I trust Jesus."

Shockingly, Bishop continued to say, "Well, if you love Jesus and trust Jesus, then all that's going on with you and the concerns for your husband, isn't nothing but, "DRAMA, DRAMA, DRAMA!"

Before leaving Bishop's office, he informed me that the real problem was that I really **DID NOT BELIEVE** that God was going to **DO** what He **SAYS** in his word (Bible) he would do for those who are bound by the enemy with addictions, sickness, disease, etc.

Finally, Bishop told me to leave my concerns about my husband with God and stop going back picking them up myself and trying to do it **MY** way. Meanwhile, he told me to treat my husband good and go on with my life because there was nothing else I could do for my husband.

Act Three
An Eye, Ear, and Mouth Opener

WOW!! Did my eyes, ears, and mouth open wide after hearing Bishop Caldwell, I FELT, refer to me as a "DRAMA QUEEN!" I could not stop laughing at what he said. Everyone that knows Bishop can testify that he has such a great sense of humor with how he uses his words to get you to understand what God gives him to reveal to you.

No MORE DRAMA

Act Four
A Moment of Humiliation

Now, it's time for me to go home. My work day ended at 5:00 p.m. After leaving the church and heading for home, my FLESH kicked into OVERDRIVE and I began to feel HUMILIATED! Between my initial laughter and later humiliation, I said to myself, "I Can't Believe that Bishop in his own way, TO MY FACE, called me a DRAMA QUEEN!

(I must admit at this point, I could qualify as a BONAFIDE CERTIFIED DRAMA QUEEN). All this time I've been thinking that my husband was the PROBLEM. Not So!

The Holy Spirit, who knows all things and reveals them to us believers, had Bishop Caldwell speak to me and open my spiritual eyes and ears and realize that I had a Greater Problem than my husband. You ask what that problem is - - the problem of "UNBELIEF".

No MORE DRAMA

Act Five
A Sleeping, Creeping, Spirit

Here again, I COULD NOT BELIEVE IT!! I asked myself, "How was it that the Spirit of unbelief was sleeping and creeping inside of me?" I told myself, "This could not be". You see, so many times in my life I have trusted and believed God and he has come through for me! Needless to say, since meeting with Bishop Caldwell, I have stopped and actually looked over my life and the things I do and have done to see if **UNBELIEF** in my life is the Real Problem and not just my husband.

No MORE DRAMA

GUILT..., GUILTY..., GUILTY

The VERDICT IS IN! I'M FOUND GUILTY!

I found out after assessing my life I, have BELIEVED God for
SOME things, but not for ALL Things. For example, I believed
and trusted God to bring my only son back home safely after he
served in the Armed Forces for eight months in the war against
Iraq. But believing God for my husband's deliverance from
alcohol addiction is quite challenging!

Unknowingly, as a result of this halfhearted belief, i.e. believing
God for **Some** things and not for **All** things, I allowed the spirit
of unbelief to lie Dormant inside of me and then awaken and
start creeping and moving into all situations that I was trying to
do myself and not totally trusting God to do for me. Lets take a
15 minute intermission during this play and examine the word.
"DORMANT". According to Webster's Ninth New Collegiate

Dictionary, Dormant means temporarily in abeyance
(temporarily inactive),yet capable of being activated or resumed.
Thus, you see, as I allowed myself to half believe God, i.e.
believe for some situations and circumstances in my life but not
all, the spirit of UNBELIEF that was lying dormant or
temporarily inactive, was activated or came alive in my mind,
body, soul, and spirit for the things I was trying to do on my own
and in my own way and not totally believing God to do.

No MORE DRAMA

As a result of the spirit of UNBELIEF being activated or coming out of its dormant state, I started disbelieving and acting out in all areas of my life, marriage, home, and even in the work place. In other words I became a "DRAMA QUEEN". In Hebrews 3:12 (KJV) warns us "Take heed, brethren, lest there be in any of you an evil heart of **Unbelief** in departing from the living God". Let's continue this 15 minute intermission in this play and examine the word **"HEED"**, that the writer in Hebrews warns us to take. According to Webster's Ninth New Collegiate Dictionary, HEED means to pay attention to; give consideration or attention to; mind; study; an awareness.

Therefore, you as the reader as well as myself the author need to take heed i.e. pay attention, study, consider, be concerned, concentrate and be aware of all circumstances and situations in our lives and make sure that we are believing God for ALL circumstances and situations in our lives and not just SOME. I believe that by giving attention to and being mindful of whether we are believing God or not believing God, can save us from the destructive results of UNBELIEF that can rob us of our joy, peace, sleep, health, wealth, stability in our marriage and everything good that God has promised for our lives. John 10:10 (KJV), reminds us that, "The thief cometh not but to steal, and to kill and to destroy... I am come that they might have life and that **they might have it more abundantly"**. **Certainly the Spirit of** UNBELIEF can be considered a thief that comes to steal, kill and destroy a person's life and dreams. Remember unbelief lies dormant on the inside of you and when it is activated by not believing God for all things, it starts moving and creeping in every area of your life.

Throughout the Bible other supporting scriptures shines light on the consequences of having UNBELIEF: Hebrews 3:17 tells us that after Moses brought the children of Israel out of Egypt, that some of them COULD NOT ENTER THE PROMISE LAND because of UNBELIEF; Jude 1:5 TELLS US, "I WILL THEREFORE PUT YOU IN REMEMBRANCE THOUGH YE ONCE KNEW THIS, HOW THAT THE Lord having saved the people out of the land of Egypt, afterward DESTROYED them that BELIEVED NOT". Thus, just as the children of Israel back in those days could not enter their Promise Land due to UNBELIEF neither can we today enter into the Promises that God has for us if we have UNBELIEF. Also, we too, can literally be destroyed eternally for not believing God for our Salvation. Romans 10:9 (KJV) clearly states that if thou shalt confess with thou mouth the Lord Jesus, and shalt BELIEVE in thine heart that God has raised him from the dead, thou shalt be saved. For with the heart man BELIEVETH unto righteousness; and with the mouth confession is made unto salvation.

No MORE DRAMA

Act Seven
Got to Kill it and Kill it Dead

Therefore, as a Born Again, Sanctified, Holy Ghost Filled,
Tongue Talking, Scripture Quoting, Bible Toting Believer, I've
GOT TO CHANGE!!!!   I MUST CHANGE what I've been
doing because I don't ever want the spirit of UNBELIEF ever to
abide within me again and cause all that DRAMA in my life. I
got to kill UNBELIEF in my life and kill it dead!! How can
UNBELIEF be killed? I feel we can kill UNBELIEF in three
ways:

1. with our HEARTS
2. with our TONGUES
3. with our LIFESTYLE

First, killing Unbelief with your **heart** takes center stage because
whatever is in your heart will come out of your mouth. Matthew
12:34 (KJV) states, "Out of the abundance of the heart the mouth
speaketh". If we study God's word and meditate on it day and
night, we will have it in our hearts and we can BELIEVE God's
word and speak it out of our mouth.
Secondly, we can kill Unbelief with our **tongue.** Proverbs 18:21
(KJV) tells us that death and life are in the power of the tongue
and they that love it (life) shall eat the fruit thereof. Thus, if we
speak the word of God that we **BELIEVE**, we shall have what
the word of God says we can have.
Thirdly, we can kill Unbelief by **living out our lives** according
to the word of God. Galatians 2:20 (KJV) states, "I am crucified

with Christ, nevertheless I live; yet not I, but Christ liveth in me and the life which I now live in the flesh I live by the faith (BELIEF) of the Son of God. In addition, Romans1:17 (KJV) states....the just shall live by faith (BELIEF) and Acts 17:28 (KJV) states....For in Him we live, and move and have our being. Therefore, to put it in a nut shell, one can kill UNBELIEF and kill it dead by:

Believing in your heart the word of God, CONFESSING with your mouth the word of God and Living out your life according to the word of God.

Act Eight

Repent and Renew your Mind

As a result of my being made aware of my possessing the spirit of UNBELIEF, I have repented before the Lord and renewed my mind daily in his word. Both my life and marriage have taken a turn for the better. Thus, I see things differently now. Instead of my husband being changed for now, I Have Changed! My circumstances with my husband haven't changed yet in the physical, But I HAVE CHANGED by BELIEVING and RENEWING my mind by the word of God and APPLYING God's word in all areas of my life and marriage. As a result of my TOTAL BELIEF and APPLICATION of God's word in my marriage, I have been strengthened spiritually, physically and mentally to deal with my circumstances until God in his own timing manifest my husband's deliverance from his addiction. I will see the glory of God in my husband's deliverance because just as Jesus said unto Martha after the death of her brother Lazarus who he would raise from the dead, " John 11:40…said I not unto thee, that if thou wouldest BELIEVE thou shouldest see the glory of God?" i.e. Lazarus being raised from the dead.

Meanwhile, I will see the glory of God revealed in my husband's deliverance as I totally believe God for his almighty healing and delivering power. Therefore, I will no longer allow the spirit of UNBLIEF to sleep and creep in my body, because I will BELIEVE God's word for **All** things and not just **Some** things.

24

No MORE DRAMA

Act Nine

CURTAIN CLOSES

At last, I, Drama Queen Linda, have less drama in my life than before. Prayerfully, as I walk in the wisdom of God and **Believe** wholeheartedly his precious anointed word all of the time for All things, and apply his word daily in my life, my reactions to life will be completely void of **DRAMA** and filled with all the wonderful promises that God has given to us believers.

There are two Lessons For A Lifetime I have learned as this play comes to its finality: First, when you believe God for some things and not all things, you set yourself up to allow the spirit of UNBELIEF to live within you and cause you to go through all kinds of changes i.e. DRAMA. Secondly, our BELIEF in God and his faithful word has to be a **Daily Lifestyle of Believing and Acting on what we Believe and not a DRESS REHERSAL i.e. putting God and his word on for SOME things and TAKING HIM OFF for others.**

No MORE DRAMA

Act Ten
Conclusion Epilogue

In conclusion, even though this book is small, I feel it carries a **BIG MESSAGE**: Possessing the "Spirit of Unbelief" can cause all kinds of Drama in your life. Even though this book shares a little humor, please take serious the truth about possessing the spirit of UNBELIEF. Take an intermission in your life and daily activities and evaluate and see if you have allowed or presently allowing the spirit of UNBELIEF to sleep and creep within you. If you find out that you are harboring "Unbelief", PRAY AND REPENT. If you pray in all sincerity and BELIEVE in God's word, and ACT on it, the HOLY SPIRIT, who is our helper, will began to work in your life just as it did in mine and transform you into the BELIEVER that God created you to be!

Be Blessed, be Delivered and have no more UNBELIEF, thus "NO MORE DRAMA!"

Now it's your time to make a list of the things in your life that are causing you to be a DRAMA Queen or DRAMA King.

1.

2.

3.

4.

5.

6.

7.

8.

9.

10.

No MORE DRAMA

Now it's your time to make a list of the things in your life that are causing you to walk in UNBELIEF.

1.

2.

3.

4.

5.

6.

7.

8.

9.

10.

No MORE DRAMA

About the Author

Linda Allen Caldwell is a 63 year old female; she is the wife of the late Nathaniel Caldwell Jr., who was her 10th grade high school sweetheart. Also, she is the proud mother of three adult children, Renee, Michael, and Shelly, as well as the proud grandmother of two delightful granddaughters Bria Sinclair and Nya-Simone.

Mrs. Caldwell loved English and writing from her young childhood and throughout high school and college.

The desire to begin writing small spiritual books was ignited from within by the Holy Spirit's power to bring out of her, all the talent and skills that she already possesses. Her messages are sent from above.

No MORE DRAMA

In Memory of My Loving Husband

Psalm 100 (King James Version)

Make a joyful noise unto the Lord, all ye lands. Serve the Lord with gladness: come before his presence with singing, Know ye that the Lord he is God: it is he that hath made us, and not we ourselves: we are his people, and the sheep of his pasture. Enter into his gates with thanksgiving, and into his courts with praise: be thankful unto him, and bless his name. For the Lord is good; his mercy is everlasting, and his truth endureth to all generations.

Psalm 100 is the scripture that the Holy Spirit spoke to my spirit the morning of November 1, 2014, as I had my morning meditation and prayer time with the Lord, before my husband's demise.

Sometimes when I am meditating and studying God's word, the Holy Spirit makes some verse stand out more than others. Thus, verse 3 of Psalm 100 stood out: "Know ye that the Lord he is God; it is he that has made us, and not we ourselves; we are his people, and the sheep of his pasture".

Little did I know as my husband laid asleep in the bed before his demise, the Lord was already preparing me for his demise less than an hour later.

Therefore, I decided to add a section in my book in memory of my husband because my book "NO MORE DRAMA –A LESSON FOR A LIFETIME" shared much meaning about a portion of his life.

Even though my husband's addiction to alcohol, mentioned earlier in the book had stopped, it was his 2-3 month short fight with throat cancer that caused his demise.

Did my husband's death cause me to become a DRAMA QUEEN all over again and possess the SPIRIT of UNBELIEF all over again like I did when starting to write this book?

NO MAM! NO SIR!

From the time I started writing this book and being made aware that I had the SPIRIT of UNBELIEF dwelling in me, I repented before the Lord and started believing God for ALL things and not just SOME Things.

Certainly, I prayed and believed God for my husband's healing just as I did for his deliverance from alcohol addiction. But, God is the God of ALL WISDOM! Thus, when the HOLY SPIRIT had me to focus on vs 3 of Psalm 100 the morning of my husband's death, I feel, that God in all his <u>sovereignty</u> was preparing and reminding me that my husband belong to him, he made my husband, my husband didn't make himself, neither did I make him or myself! In verse 4 of Psalm 100 I was reminded to enter into his gates with thanksgiving and into his courts with praise, be thankful unto him, and bless his name, verse 5 of Psalm 100 also reminded me that the Lord is good, his mercy is everlasting; and his truth endureth to all generations.

Therefore, here again I choose to believe God and his word for ALL things and not just SOME so I want have to have all kinds of drama going on with my Life and Health because of my husband's departure.

In conclusion, I truly miss my husband because I loved him for 41 years of marriage and we were high school sweethearts from the 10th – 12th grade and throughout college. I know my husband accepted Jesus into his life because I offered the plan of salvation to him in Romans10:9-10 back in the year 2001.

As believers, we all know that II Corinthians 5:8 tells us…to be absent from the body is to be present with the Lord.

Therefore, I will stand on God's word and do what he tells me to do in Psalm 100 verse 4-5 "Enter into his gates with thanksgiving and into his courts with praise, be thankful unto him, and bless his name, For the Lord is good, his mercy is everlasting; and his truth endureth to all generations".

I will forever thank God for my husband's life and our courtship and 41 years of marriage and continually thank him every day for my forward move in my life and trusting and believing him for all things at all times and not allow the SPIRIT OF UNBELIEF to dwell in me and rob me of my Joy, Peace, Health, Wealth, etc.

Be BLESSED, Be DELIVERED and have no more UNBELIEF, thus" NO MORE DRAMA"

No MORE DRAMA

No MORE DRAMA

No MORE DRAMA

Back Cover

No More Drama

A Lesson For A Life Time

Are you a BELIVER?

Are you walking around with UNBELIEF?

Do you have the title of DRAMA QUEEN?

Do you have the title of DRAMA KING?

I WAS A DRAMA QUEEN

If you are not sure of the answers to the above questions then this book is a must for you to read. It will tell you if you are a DRAMA QUEEN or a DRAMA KING. It will let you know for sure if you are walking around with UNBELIFE in your life.

This book is a must read for the young, the old as well as the middle age individuals.

ISBN 978-0-9861274-0-3 $5.00 U.S.
$10.00 Can.

www.ingramcontent.com/pod-product-compliance
Lightning Source LLC
Chambersburg PA
CBHW022348040426
42449CB00006B/776